Introduction

'Trees are keen to tell us so much.
They'll tell us about the land, the water, the people, the animals, the weather and time.
And they will tell us about their lives, the good bits and the bad.
Trees tell a story, but only to those who know how to read it.'

The Art of Reading Trees by Tristan Gooley.

Chapter 1
July 2024

An oak tree cannot walk, but after 50 years has had 10 000 000 children called Acorns.

Imagine being 50 and having 10 000 000 children around your feet!

But this never happens, mostly because of one animal: Squirrel.

During September to November every Squirrel will bury 50 Acorns every 60 minutes for about 90 days!

There are 140 000 Red Squirrels and 2.5 million Grey Squirrels in the UK.

You do the maths!

The Acorns are buried in special hiding places far away from the tree.

These will be dug up again in the Winter months for food.

But Squirrel can be forgetful and about 30% of all buried Acorn hoards are left in the ground and one of these might, MIGHT start to grow.

Any lying on the floor may be eaten by Squirrel, Badger, Deer, Jay, Mouse, Fox and/or Human.

Chapter 2
January 1798

A hoard of 27 Acorns lay buried near the bottom of a slope of a pasture deep in the countryside in South East Hampshire.

Squirrel has not returned during the Winter for its feast.

Most Acorns have rotted.

However the Soil is favourable and something stirs amongst the worms, nutrients and minerals.

One of the Acorns has rolled over and a tiny root has emerged with instructions to dig deep and spread.

It grips and spreads amongst the Soil gratefully drinking the water and drawing up the minerals and nutrients.

It feels good.

At its other end one shoot emerges from the Soil into the atmosphere and warmth of the Sun.

Genetic instructions are streaming to its root and its shoot as it strives to thrive and survive.

A baby Oak is born, far away from its parent but it can feel the Sun and chilly Wind.

The Oak cannot walk, but it can think, feel, sense, talk (if you listen carefully), it can drink through its roots and with a little sparkle of sunlight can eat and grow.

Oak sees everything and the taller it gets the more it sees and the more other animals are attracted to it.

Oak doesn't need to turn around because it can see 360 degrees.

Oak doesn't miss a thing.

Chapter 3
1802-1820

I'm 4 years old! Happy birthday me!

Some news: things, and I'm not quite sure what, are happening in the pasture here.

I heard from Woodpecker that young Oaks were being uprooted from around the Forests and were being replanted in straight lines.

Strange Human activity.

Owl explained that old straight Oaks were being chopped down and were to be used for large fighting ships which were built at a nearby city harbour called Portsmouth.

16ft lengths of straight Oak are needed for ship building.

A few months later all the men with their chopping tools had left the pasture and that night we had a small celebration, away from the Humans.

Squirrel told me that evening that someone called William Garrett had bought a farmhouse nearby and all its grounds which included the pasture in which I grew.

Within a couple of years a large renovated house had been built across the track and Purple Hairstreak told me that a fence had been 'planted' and now 400 acres of land is enclosed within it.

I now live in a place with a name: Leigh Park.

I hope the planted fence doesn't upset my Deer friends.

They love to roam.

Fox says that William wants to change the area into a Pleasure Ground, called a Ferme Ornee.

I'm now 22 and the pasture is changing for ever.

Ferme Ornee is a French word and means Ornamental Farm: a country estate laid out according to aesthetic principles and partly for farming.

Chapter 4
1820-1860

Late one night in 1820, Bat, who lived with me now, along with Squirrel, Owl, Purple Hairstreak and Woodpecker, came and told me that a man called George Staunton now owned all the land and liked a faraway land called China.

He built a huge White House at the farm across the track and by the time I was 40 in 1828 had started to build lots of other buildings, much smaller, around me.

A Temple of Friendship, and very close to me, a Shell House decorated with shells and pebbles from Hayling Beach.

Squirrel was very upset because a new pebble pathway was being built for the Shell House and I seemed to be in the way!

But I wasn't!

I saw an Ice Pond and an Ice House built which would supply Staunton with small frozen lumps of water.

At the bottom of the pasture slope where it flattened out many trees, bushes and flowers of all types were dug up.

I don't know where they went, but a huge 3.5 acre hole was left.

This eventually filled with water and loads of different fish lived in it.

Even more amazing was the arrival of many flying friends: Seagull, Duck, Moorhen, Swan, Heron and Kingfisher.

They loved it there and it was wonderful to watch them and hear their calls.

Chapter 4
1820-1860

Its a very busy period and around my 40th birthday new roads, tracks, pathways and even a couple of Lodges were built.

Work continued on the formation of the Lake and news came from Owl that as he hunted in the night Staunton's house was entirely white and looked like a crouching ghost.

It was built over at the farm.

Sparrow told of beautiful colonnades and a conservatory where exotic fruit like pineapples, pears and apricots grew.

An octagonal Gothic Library was added and back over here a Beacon with a flag on top appeared along with a Turkish tea house and an Obelisk, which could be seen for miles.

Chapter 4
1820-1860

During this period a lot of people were enjoying the grounds: gentleman and ladies walking together whilst their children ran everywhere, shouting and laughing, exploring and studying.

They gasped at the Lake with its shimmering beauty and evolving bird life.

Sometimes, if it was hot, families would sit under my branches in the shade, drinking lemonade and eating apples and cake. Lots of children would hug me, climb me and feel my bark and talk to me asking so many questions:

'How old are you?'

'How long have you been here?'

'Do you have any acorns?'

'Do lots of other animals live with you?'

'Do you like cake?'

'Where do you go at night time?'

'Can you sleep?'

'Can you hear me?'

'Will you be here forever?'

Well, I knew most of the answers of course, but I think its better if they find out for themselves and write the answers in the gaps above.

Chapter 4
1820-1860

The Lake was becoming an incredible sight and men talked of all the fish living in it. Islands were created in the Lake: Fort Island, Swan Island and Cottage Island.

Bridges were constructed so people could get to the Islands: the Chinese Bridge and the Corinthian Bridge, a Boathouse, a green arbour and an impressive hexagonal Chinese Summer House.

In addition, by my 40th birthday, a Cross House, a Moss House and a Lookout were completed.

A lovely gentleman called Joseph would regularly cycle up to me, lean his bicycle against my trunk and get out his easel and lots of beautiful colours to paint what he could see.

He would always say 'Thank you Oak' when he left.

Chapter 4
1820-1860

Around this time,amidst all this activity I suddenly felt very weary.

Weirdly I felt that I might be dying although I'd never felt so alive.

I spoke to Squirrel whose unabashed excitement left me puzzled.

'Acorns', Squirrel squealed, 'you're growing Acorns'!

Squirrel was correct and at the age of 40 I gave birth to 2,200 of them!

Eventually everyone of them fell to the ground. Squirrel, Badger, Jay, Mouse and Fox all sampled some and Squirrel was very busy carrying hundreds and hundreds away and burying them for Winter food just like me in 1798.

An Oak may produce over a million Acorns during its lifetime. Each single acorn could then produce another million.

Chapter 4
1820-1860

As if things couldn't get anymore exciting a beautiful lady appeared, standing on the far side of the Lake on an area called Temple Lawn.

She looked across the Lake with her silver bow and arrow that gleams and sparkles in the sunlight.

Owl informed us all that this was a statue of the Goddess Diana.

She is Goddess of the Moon and of the hunt, the woods and the forests.

Sometimes, very special times, when it is dark but the sky is cloudless, I can see a crescent moon in the sky behind her.

Quite wonderful.

Chapter 4
1820-1860

Jay reports that a Dutch garden is being created near the White House, plus a Cone House, an Iron House and a Swiss House.

I wonder who lives in them all.

A long curly pathway has come into my view which Deer says is called the Serpentine Walk.

All the commotion and building frenzy came to a halt and it wasn't until 10 years and 20000 Acorns later that news came from Deer of an incredible Tropical Lily House built very near to the White House.

Its 1853, I'm 55 and have so many admiring visitors that it makes me very happy.

Staunton seems to have created a place out of the farm and this pasture that people of all ages love to visit and stay for hours.

Children talk to me all the time and climb on my boughs and lie on them or against my trunk in the grass.

Chapter 4
1820-1860

Once an old shuffling Lady came towards me.

She looked a bit muddy and her hands looked as if they had done a lot of work.

It was strange to see her out because it was night, but very clear, enabling the moonlight to share its magical hue over all it saw.

She had a wicker basket tucked over her arm and I could glimpse lots of herbs and flower parts in it.

She carefully rested the basket down at my trunk and with one palm stretched out and pressing upon my trunk, closed her eyes and spoke:

Greetings of love and gratitude

Oh blessed Oak
Sacred soul
Ancient soul

Release some bark to me
So I may use your healing powers
My soul to you
Goddess Diana and Mother Earth

Blessed Be

Chapter 4
1820-1860

Old Lady took a shiny tool from the basket and picked away until she had a couple of small strips of bark.

She thanked me each time and told me that she would dry the bark, shred it and boil it in water.

With this she would bathe her husband's eczema.

It would soothe and heal the condition.

It would also cure his sweaty feet and piles!

I was only too happy to help.

Some of it she added she would dry for him to chew because when he did it put him off alcohol.

There were some acorns still lying around and she gathered some of these and thanking me told me that she would peel them, roast them and then grind them into a powder from which a lovely hot Winter drink was made.

I watched her walk off on the Serpentine Path with her basket.

I wondered if she was the Goddess Diana.

Chapter 4
1820-1860

Around 1858, when I was 60, on another moonlit night a couple of young people, friends of Staunton approached me.

They began gathering Acorns and danced and skipped happily around my trunk, sometimes holding hands, sometimes not.

Owl whispered to me that they believed that gathering acorns in Moonlight would give them incredible fertility powers.

They are planning to have children, Owl concluded.

'Well I've had about 45000 of them' I replied.

The couple left but unlike Old Lady never spoke to me, touched me or thanked me.

Still, good luck to them!

Chapter 4
1820-1860
August 10th 1859

Next morning, the Sun forced the mist to rise

The birds began their chorus of thanks and joyfulness.

Some devastating news emerged.

Sir George Thomas Staunton had died.

Chapter 5
1859-1875

Further updates over the following weeks revealed that a man named William Stone had bought the whole estate and had already started demolishing the White House.

However, between 1859 and 1861 an extraordinary sight occurred; just up the rise from me, on the flat plateau towards the East, an enormous brick Swiss style Gothic mansion was built.

It stares out towards the Lake, blocking my early morning Sunlight and warmth.

However, I've sent a message to my Apical to stretch higher and to the Purple Hairstreaks to move up with it.

Deer says that Stone had built two big brick kilns to the north of the Lake and dug out enough clay to make and fire over one million bricks to construct it.

By 1865, my 67th birthday, a new Coach House and stables had been built.

A Wellhouse complex has been placed where fresh water was captured, managed, manipulated and transported via a well, tanks and a reservoir up the steep slope to the mansion.

Chapter 5
1859-1875

Amongst all the noise and activity I had noticed that the Goddess Diana statue no longer glinted in the sunlight.

Sparrow is concerned that she is ill as she is slowly turning green.

Squirrel and Fox both add that a number of Staunton's smaller buildings around the Lake and elsewhere are beginning to look untidy and discoloured.

Stone however, has:
Peaches
Pears,
Pineapples
Apples and
Apricots; some growing on trees or in pits within the new Storey Gardens.

The sound of the coaches and horses continues to fill the daytime air and an increasing number of people are spending time here again, enjoying the surroundings.

Chapter 5
1859-1875

A couple, smartly dressed and with arms linked, stood below my large lowest bough, and began a conversation.

The man, very much wanting to impress the lady filled her with fascinating facts:

The whole estate now covers 200 acres.

There are 650 trees on the estate.

There are 85 different species of tree.

The lady, noticeably unimpressed with fascinating facts and wanting terribly to be loved as much as an Oak, nevertheless listened politely as he turned and addressed me directly.

' And this wonderful Oak my dear'
he temporarily released his arm and leant against me,

' has over 2300 fauna and flora species associated with it and indeed...'
he paused and glanced up through my boughs and branches encouraging her to do likewise,

'up there somewhere are 300 species relying entirely on this one Oak for their own survival.'

They wandered off towards the Shell House and down the cobbled path.

They linked arms again.

Chapter 5
1859-1875

Stone was clearly a very social man who wanted to share this paradise with others.

For many years some fantastic parties were thrown.

Thousands of the public from his constituency of Portsmouth were allowed access to enjoy the grounds in late Spring and Summer.

In the Winter when the Lake froze people of all ages would scream hysterically and slide, fall and skate across it.

There was a very happy atmosphere here with the Stone family.

He was MP for Portsmouth from 1865 to 1874, but, having failed to be re-elected, William Henry Stone moved away from the area forever.

Chapter 6
1875 -1920

The mansion was bought by a man called Lieutenant-General Sir Frederick Wellington John Fitzwygham who moved in with his family.

I was now 77 years old.

Few additions were made to the house or the estate.

Sparrow learnt that Fitzwygham was the English Army's horse expert and commanded a Cavalry brigade.

In 1898 Frederick, his son, aged 14 was sent to a special school called Eton.

A group of young men sat beneath my boughs and discussed the School.

What really excited the men, however, was news of the imminent formation of a professional Football Club inaugurated in the ever expanding city of nearby Portsmouth.

One of the young men was explaining the advantages of investing in this very modern enterprise.

Chapter 6
1875-1920

I had noticed, as the years passed that a lot of the shrubs, bushes and plants, once so lovingly cared for by the Head Gardener and his large estate staff under Staunton, were now overgrown and growing wild and unmaintained.

During Fitzwygham's time my trunk was slowly being surrounded by increasingly thick and impenetrable pinky purple bushes called Rhododendron.

In 1904 Fitzwygham died and his son, Frederick, now aged 20 took over the estate.

Chapter 6
1875-1920

When Frederick was 30 years old he attended an overseas event that Owl described as a Great War.

Thousands and thousands of young men went from the area.

Thousands never returned home..

One who did return was Frederick who despite a shrapnel head wound received at a place called Ypres distinguished himself with much bravery.

Over 30 countries sent their men and young boys to the Great War.

Approximately 40 million died.

Chapter 6
1875-1920

Whilst he was away at war, his ailing mother Lady Fitzwygham and his sister Angela remained at the mansion.

Late one stormy night a group of four men, dressed in dark clothes and heavily cowled, ran from the mansion down towards me where they paused, looked back at the mansion and cowered, half hidden within the tangle of a feral Rhododendron.

They had between them two sacks and two spades.

The sacks rattled as they placed them roughly to the ground.

Two men dug feverishly whilst the other two kept an anxious eye on the mansion.

A large hole appeared, the sacks were dropped in it and the soil, clay and leaves were placed over them and packed in tightly.

The men, whispering and in an increasing state of panic left the area, running towards the old decaying Shell House.

**Chapter 6
1875-1920**

What was in those sacks I don't know.

Owl informed me that Lady Fitzwygham has been burgled.

A lot of jewellery, plus miscellaneous gold and silver objects had been stolen.

If that's what was in the sacks then I have news for you.

Its still here!

Those men never returned to dig it up again.

Chapter 6
1875-1920

In the following years following his return I often saw and heard Frederick and his friends charging around the estate on horses.

Dozens of dogs ran with them chasing hares.

Fox found this very traumatic and left the area with his family.

Frederick's group were called the Leigh Park Beagles and became quite famous.

Two years after surviving the Great War with shrapnel in his head, Frederick caught The Spanish Flu and died.

Chapter 7
1920-1939

There was, Owl explained to me, no heir to the estate as Frederick had died without a son or daughter.

Angela and her mother, Lady Fitzwygham, continued to live there and would open the grounds for the public, but slowly, especially in the 1930s the decline of the once great estate began in earnest.

In late Spring of 1939, an excited visitor explained to his friend beneath my boughs that Portsmouth Football Club had won the most prestigious club competition in the world: the FACup!

If I heard correctly they'd beaten some Wolves.

By the beginning of September all the able bodied men and boys had to go abroad again to fight in another war and on September 3rd Angela, now alone since her mother's death, moved out of Leigh Park.

An era had ended.

At the age of 141 I was very worried about the future of the mansion and the gardens.

Chapter 8
1939-1945

The next Great war had started and as before, men and boys swarmed from their hamlets, villages, towns and cities to fulfill their duty and sign up.

The house, the land, the lake and the forests were all requisitioned by the Government and was used by the Admiralty Mine Design and Research Department of HMS Vernon under the stewardship of the Ministry of Defence.

Thunderous explosions were frequent and the lake threw its contents into the sky like geysers.

I wondered about the fish and birds.

Whatever this human war was, it was violent, deafening and destructive, even in this peaceful place.

The Ice House had been covered in thick concrete and the follies and buildings of Staunton were falling into desperate repair.

Green Woodpecker told me that Diana, Goddess of the Moon, the Hunt, the Woods and the Forests had left.

Her plinth remained but she had gone.

This was unnerving.

She had stood proudly in the Temple Lawn for over 100 years, glinting and winking from first light to last.

A year later the World War ended, but The Admiralty remained which meant that because they had secrets the Police guarded the estate day and night and no one, unless officially authorised, was allowed in.

Chapter 8
1939-1945

More than 50 Nations fought in WW2.

Including non-military personnel, an estimated 75 million people perished.

Chapter 9
1945-1963

Owl informed me in a rather melancholy tone that the entire estate had been sold to Portsmouth City Council, who, I assumed, would now look after everything.

The years after the war was a nervous time for all the animals and trees but in 1950 Squirrel, hanging around on the roof of the coach house heard that a Parks Committee was formed with the specific task of deciding the Estate's future.

In 1953 following a visit from many men in suits, Deer informed us all that the estate was to be designated a 'playground' and that at weekends and Bank Holidays anyone could come in and 'play'.

This was great news and it meant we had singing, dancing and laughing people around us again.

People loved being here and it filled us with joy.

In 1958 the Admiralty stated that Stone's mansion **'was not in a fit state'** and as it approached its 100th birthday and my 165th, it was demolished and pulled to the ground.

At least I could enjoy the first rays of morning light again.

Chapter 10
1963-1997

For 20 years the crowds came at weekends and bank holidays and nothing much changed.

The estate became overgrown and unloved but at least the birds and the fish of the Lake returned.

I remember Swan flying in.

In 1984 the lovely Angela Fitzwygham died peacefully in a rest home in Haslemere and with her passing the last permanent resident had gone.

She was 99 years old but left behind six beautiful water colours that she had painted from beneath my boughs.

(In 1991 they were put on display in Havant Museum for all to enjoy).

In 1987 aged 189, I was as excited as I could remember for a long time; a buzz of anticipation amongst all the creatures greeted the news, brought by Owl, that we all now lived in a place named Staunton Country Park.

A small kaleidoscope of Purple Hairstreaks danced around my canopy so relieved that it would continue to be their home as it had been for generations.

Hundreds of species celebrated all over the estate knowing that our home was safe.

Happy people in Green called Countryside Rangers spent every day for the next 20 years caring for us.

Chapter 11
2017

I'm 219 years old now and Fox told me that Chiff Chaff had listened in on a meeting in the old stables.

Chiff Chaff told Fox that the latest set of humans, still wearing Green, were celebrating.

They were clinking glasses and being very Happy.

Why?

Well, something called Lottery Funding had been granted to Staunton Country Park.

It was to be spent on Heritage and Archeology.

Staunton's Regency environment and Stone's legacy were to be celebrated, explored and mirrored as closely as possible.

I think it meant the Park would be returned to how it was when I was 22 years old.

Chapter 12
2022

As I celebrated my 224th birthday a lovely surprise occurred

A lady dressed in the Green of the Happy People stood at my trunk staring up into my canopy.

She was very happy at spotting a couple of the Purple Hairstreaks that lived up there.

I could have told her there were 15 up there but she was happy with spotting three.

Leaning in and resting upon my bark she told me that the Green Happy People called me Lady Oak.

I was famous as I was the oldest of 656 trees in the Park!

Thats 85 different Species!

I have recently spotted some Green Happy People gathered around consulting maps and digging into the ground at the Ice House, the Ice Pond, Stone's Kilns, the Well complex and most intriguingly, the area in the Temple Lawn where Diana, Moon Goddess, once stood.

Chapter 13
2023

A bearded man, one of the Green Happy People, came and talked with me every week, usually covered in mud and clay, carrying his trowel and water drink.

He stepped in close and with an 'excuse me' put his arms and a blue measuring tape around my trunk, about 2 metres from the ground.

Having measured my girth he looked at the tape and announced to me,
 'that's 245 inches, making you, Lady Oak 245 years old, therefore born in 1798.'

He gave me a hug and asked for a slither of bark to cure his sweaty feet.
.
'You've seen so much history,' he said, 'I'm going to write about everything you've seen.'

Chapter 14
2024

The gradual return of the Birds, Insects and Fish to the Lake has been marked with an incredible celebration.

Swan has had her first ever Cygnets, four in total!

The whole Park celebrates.

The Bearded Happy man in Green talks to me regularly with updates on news from the Park.

Chapter 15
2078

Am I still here?

I could be; 1000 years old is possible for us Oaks.

What else have I seen?

Has anyone continued my story?

Has the Moon Goddess returned to the Temple Lawn?

Perhaps she never went away.

The Woods, the Forests and all who live in them are still here.

The Moon still lights the night sky.

I loved it when Joseph, a friend of Staunton and Angela, daughter of Fitzwygham would set up their easels beneath my boughs and paint what they could see.

If you could come and do that I would be very happy, but if you cannot there are plenty of spaces on some pages to draw or paint what you feel.

Whatever happens; be **Green and Happy** and come and say hello to Lady Oak because one day I might not be here.

THE END?

Printed in Great Britain
by Amazon